Simply Christ

MW00785320

30 Favorite Christmas Songs and Carols

Arranged by Dan Coates

Simply Christmas is a collection of the most beloved Christmas carols and popular Christmas tunes. These songs have been carefully selected and arranged by Dan Coates for Easy Piano, making them accessible to pianists of all ages. Phrase markings, articulations, fingering, pedaling and dynamics have been included to aid with interpretation, and a large print size makes the notation easy to read.

For centuries, music has played an important part during Christmas festivities. Some traditional carols reflect on the solemnity of Christmas night, while others capture the triumphant jubilation of Jesus' arrival. Additionally, some of the more recent Christmas hits celebrate the season—the happiness of playing in the snow, and even the excitement of going on a sleigh ride. Christmas music is universally uplifting, fun to sing, and fulfilling to play. With its ability to lift our spirits and bring family and friends together, this music has been embraced by musicians and audiences, young and old, around the world. For these reasons and more, the following pages are exciting to explore.

After all, this is *Simply Christmas!*

Cover illustration by Sarah Lewis

Copyright © MMVIII by ALFRED PUBLISHING CO., INC.
All rights reserved. Printed in USA.
ISBN-10: 0-7390-5183-0
ISBN-13: 978-0-7390-5183-2

Contents

The Christmas Waltz

Words by Sammy Cahn
Music by Jule Styne
Arranged by Dan Coates

4

Angels We Have Heard on High

Traditional Carol
Arranged by Dan Coates

Away in a Manger

Traditional Carol
Arranged by Dan Coates

Slowly, with expression

The Coventry Carol

Traditional Carol
Arranged by Dan Coates

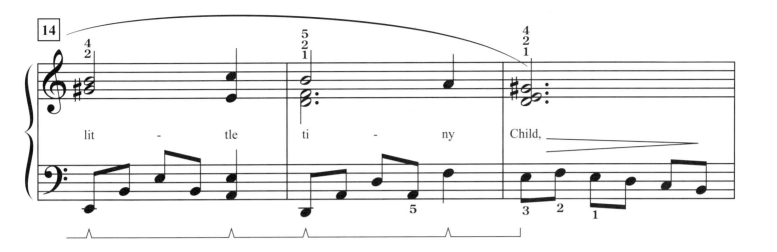

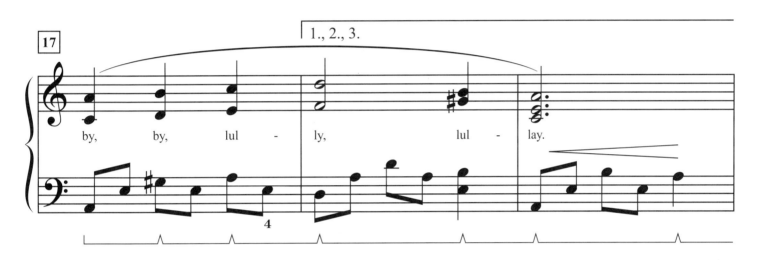

Verse 2:
O sisters, too, how may we do,
For to preserve this day
This poor youngling for whom we sing
By, by, lully, lullay.

Verse 3:
Herod the king, in his raging,
Charged he hath this day
His men of might, in his own sight,
All children young to slay.

Verse 4:
Then woe is me, poor Child, for Thee!
And ever morn and day,
For Thy parting nor say nor sing,
By, by, lully, lullay.

Deck the Hall

Traditional Carol
Arranged by Dan Coates

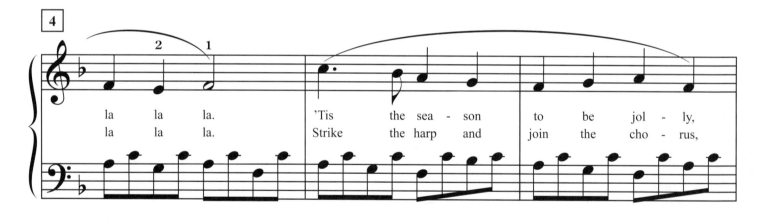

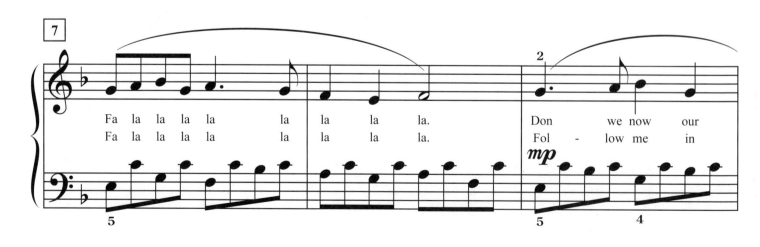

The First Noel

Traditional Carol
Arranged by Dan Coates

God Rest Ye Merry, Gentlmen

Traditional Carol
Arranged by Dan Coates

Moderately, in two

Verse 2:
In Bethlehem, in Israel, this blessed Babe was born,
And laid within a manger upon this blessed morn;
The which His mother Mary did nothing take in scorn.
(To Chorus:)

Verse 3:
From God our Heavenly Father, a blessed angel came,
And unto certain shepherds brought tidings of the same;
How that in Bethlehem was born the Son of God by name.
(To Chorus:)

Good King Wenceslas

Traditional Carol
Arranged by Dan Coates

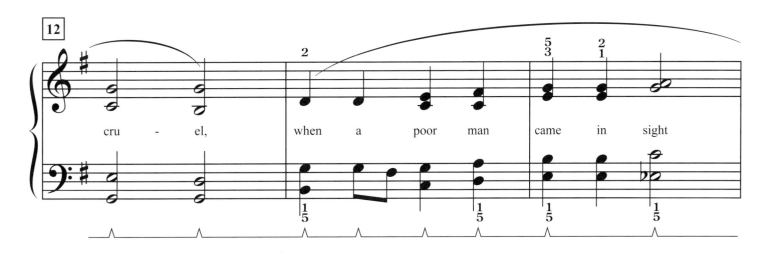

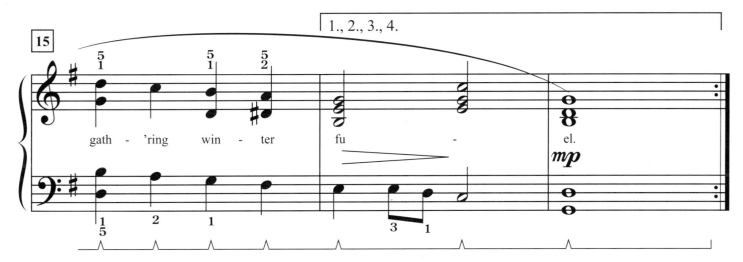

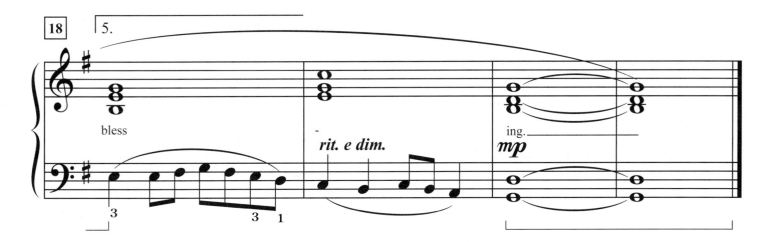

Verse 2:
"Hither, page, and stand by me, if thou know'st it, telling,
Yonder peasant, who is he? Where and what his dwelling?"
"Sire, he lives a good league hence, underneath the mountain,
Right against the forest fence, by Saint Agnes' Fountain."

Verse 3:
"Bring me flesh and bring me wine, bring me pine logs hither.
Thou and I will see him dine when we bear him thither."
Page and monarch forth they went, forth they went together,
Through the rude wind's wild lament and the bitter weather.

Verse 4:
"Sire, the night is darker now, and the wind blows stronger.
Fails my heart, I know not how, I can go no longer."
"Mark my footsteps, my good page, tread thou in them boldy.
Thou shalt find the winter's rage freeze thy blood less coldly."

Verse 5:
In his master's steps he trod, where the snow lay dinted.
Heat was in the very sod which the Saint had printed.
Therefore, Christian men, be sure, wealth or rank possessing;
Ye who now will bless the poor shall yourselves find blessing.

Frosty the Snowman

Words and Music by
Steve Nelson and Jack Rollins
Arranged by Dan Coates

Frost - y the Snow - man was a jol - ly hap - py soul, with a
Frost - y the Snow - man knew the sun was hot that day, so he

corn - cob pipe and a but - ton nose and two eyes made out of coal.
said, "Let's run and we'll have some fun now be - fore I melt a - way."

21

Hark! The Herald Angels Sing

Words and Music by Charles Wesley
Arranged by Dan Coates

24

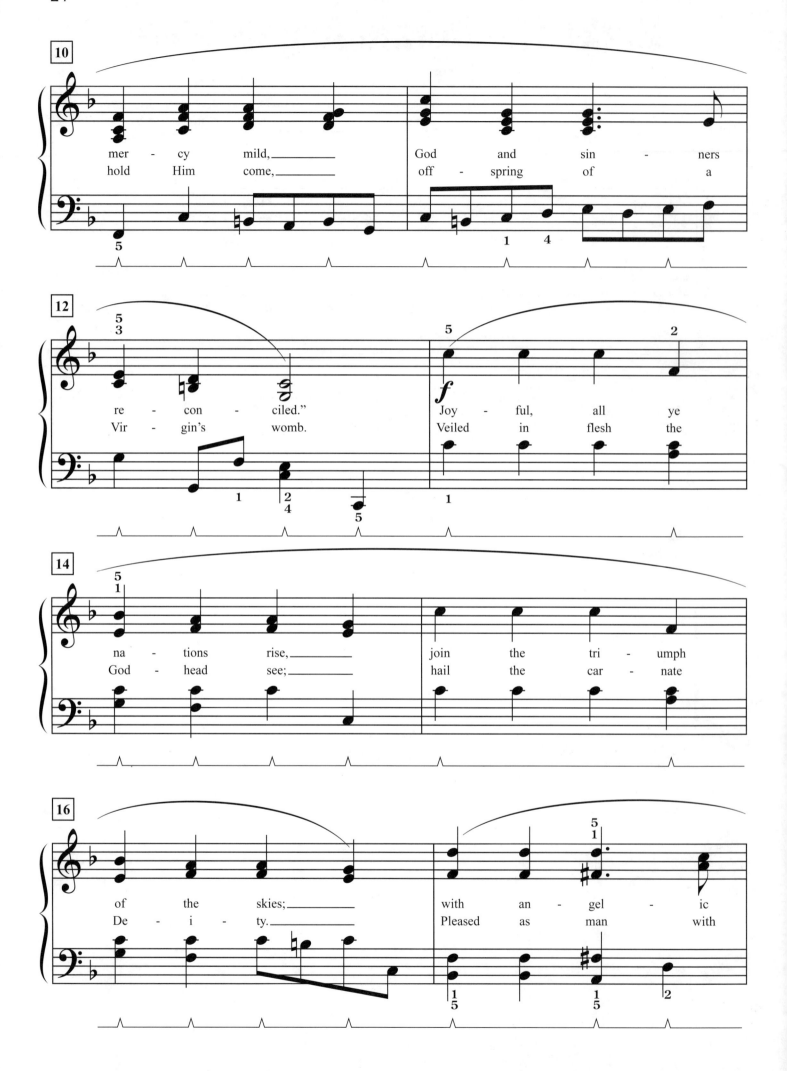

Have Yourself a Merry Little Christmas

Words and Music by
Hugh Martin and Ralph Blane
Arranged by Dan Coates

Through the years we all will be to-geth - er, if the fates al -

low. Hang a shin - ing star up - on the high - est

bough, and have your - self a

mer - ry lit - tle Christ - mas now!

(There's No Place Like)
Home for the Holidays

Words by Al Stillman
Music by Robert Allen
Arranged by Dan Coates

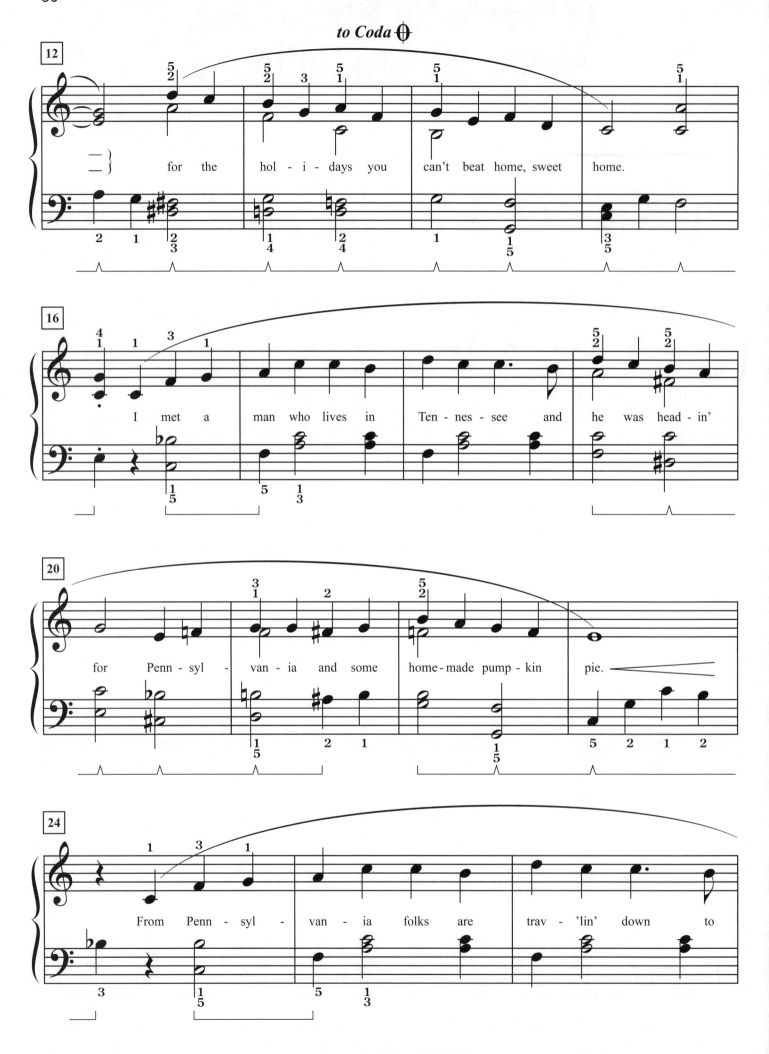

It Came Upon the Midnight Clear

Traditional Carol
Arranged by Dan Coates

It's the Most
Wonderful Time of the Year

Words and Music by
Eddie Pola and George Wyle
Arranged by Dan Coates

Jingle Bells

James Pierpont
Arranged by Dan Coates

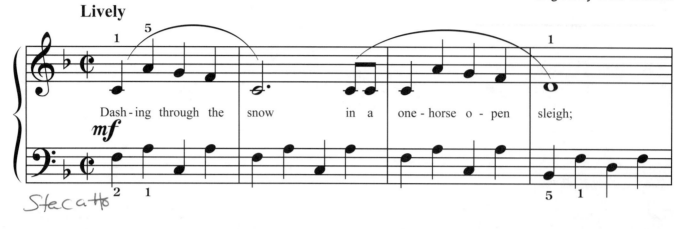

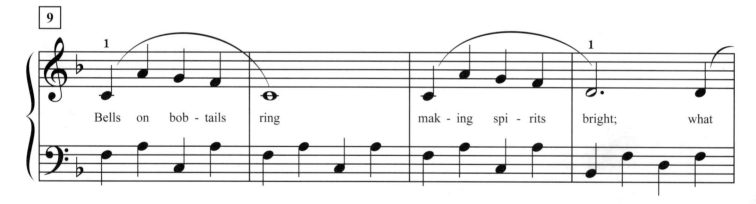

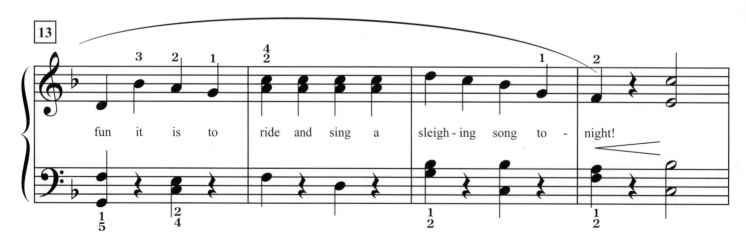

Jin - gle bells, jin - gle bells, jin - gle all the way.

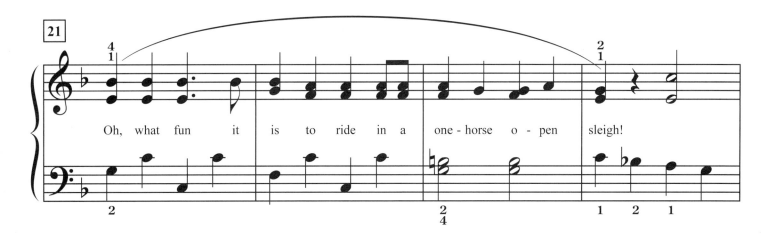

Oh, what fun it is to ride in a one - horse o - pen sleigh!

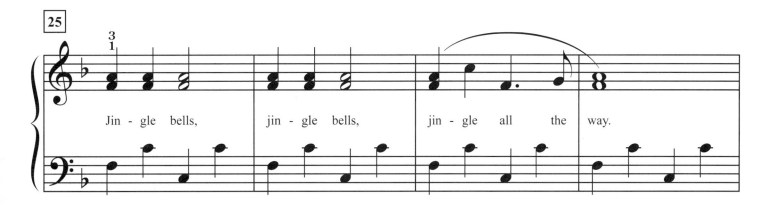

Jin - gle bells, jin - gle bells, jin - gle all the way.

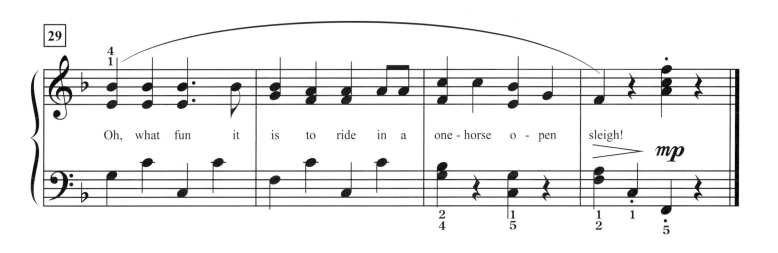

Oh, what fun it is to ride in a one - horse o - pen sleigh!

Let It Snow! Let It Snow! Let It Snow!

Words by Sammy Cahn
Music by Jule Styne
Arranged by Dan Coates

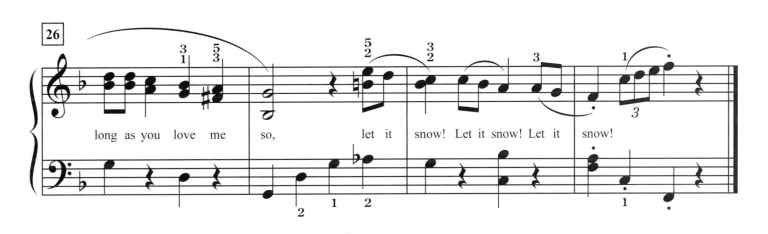

I'll Be Home for Christmas

Words by Kim Gannon
Music by Walter Kent
Arranged by Dan Coates

Slowly, with expression

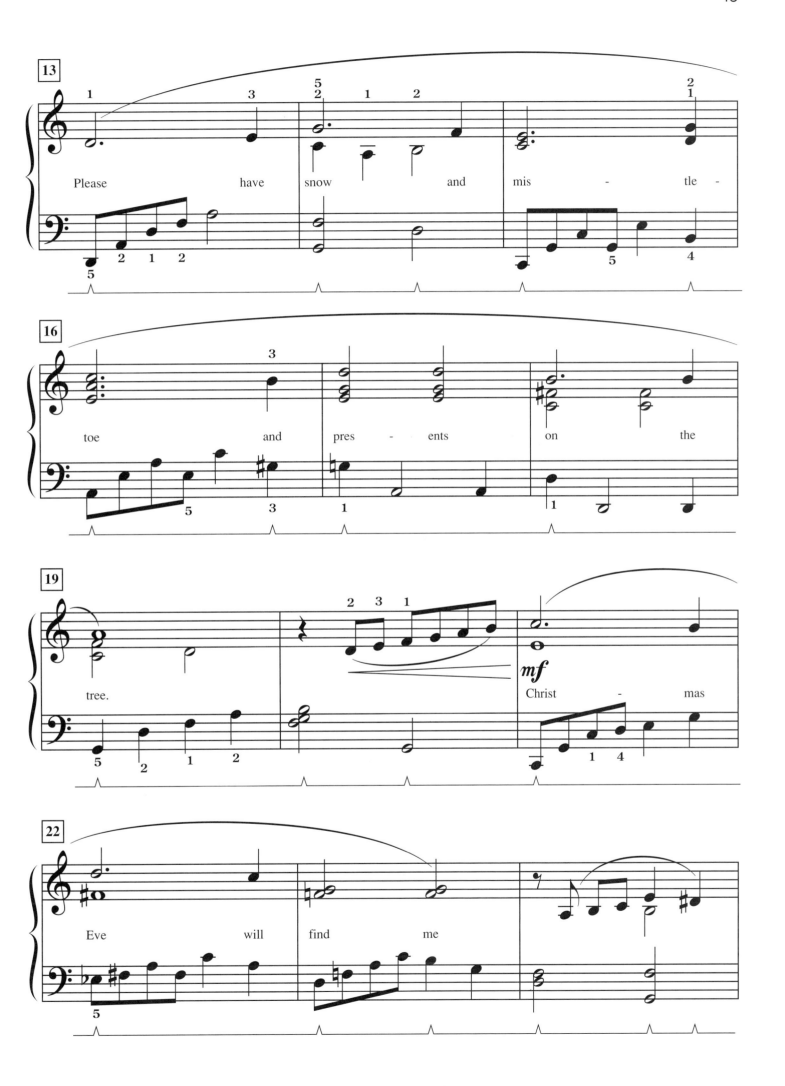

The Little Drummer Boy

Words and Music by
Harry Simeone, Henry Onorati
and Katherine Davis
Arranged by Dan Coates

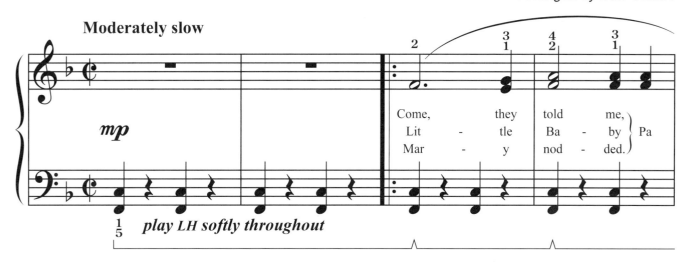

O Christmas Tree

Traditional Carol
Arranged by Dan Coates

O Come, All Ye Faithful

Traditional Carol
Arranged by Dan Coates

O Come, O Come, Emmanuel

English Lyrics by John M. Neale
Thirteenth-century Plainsong
Arranged by Dan Coates

Slowly, with reverence

O Holy Night

Words by Placide Cappeau
Music by Adolphe C. Adam
Arranged by Dan Coates

O Little Town of Bethlehem

Words by Phillips Brooks
Music by Lewis H. Redner
Arranged by Dan Coates

Santa Claus Is Coming to Town

Words by Haven Gillespie
Music by J. Fred Coots
Arranged by Dan Coates

Sleigh Ride

Words by Mitchell Parish
Music by Leroy Anderson
Arranged by Dan Coates

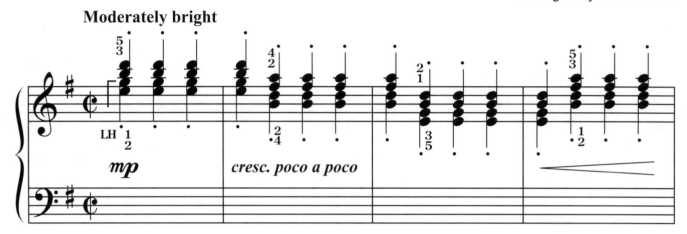

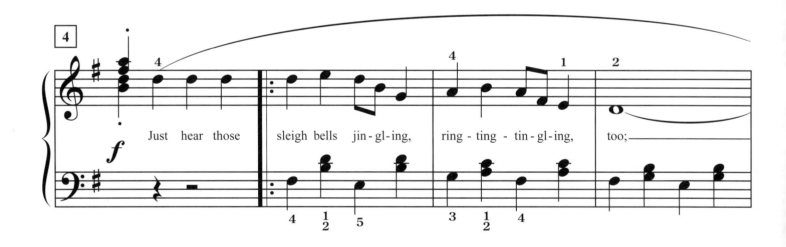

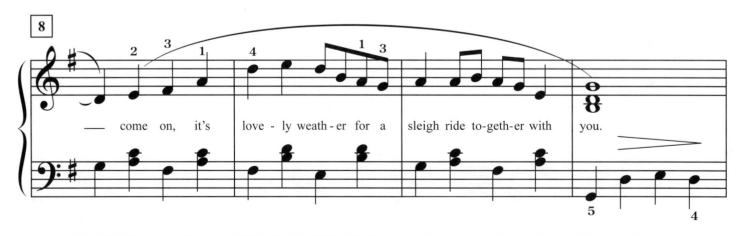

The Twelve Days of Christmas

Traditional Carol
Arranged by Dan Coates

68

Repeat as needed

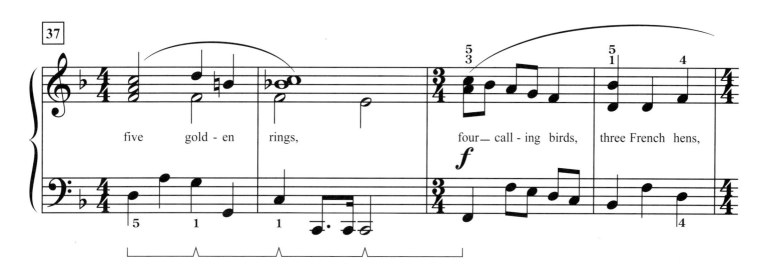

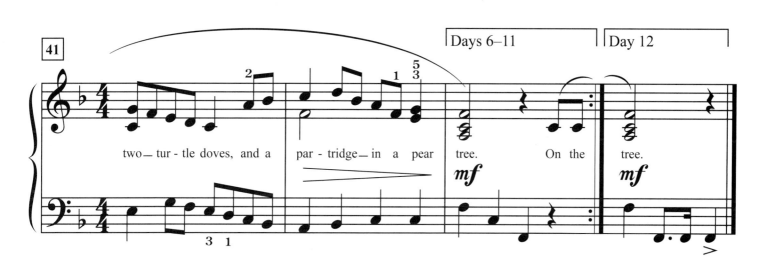

Silent Night

Words by Joseph Mohr
Music by Franz Grüber
Arranged by Dan Coates

We Three Kings of Orient Are

Traditional Carol
Arranged by Dan Coates

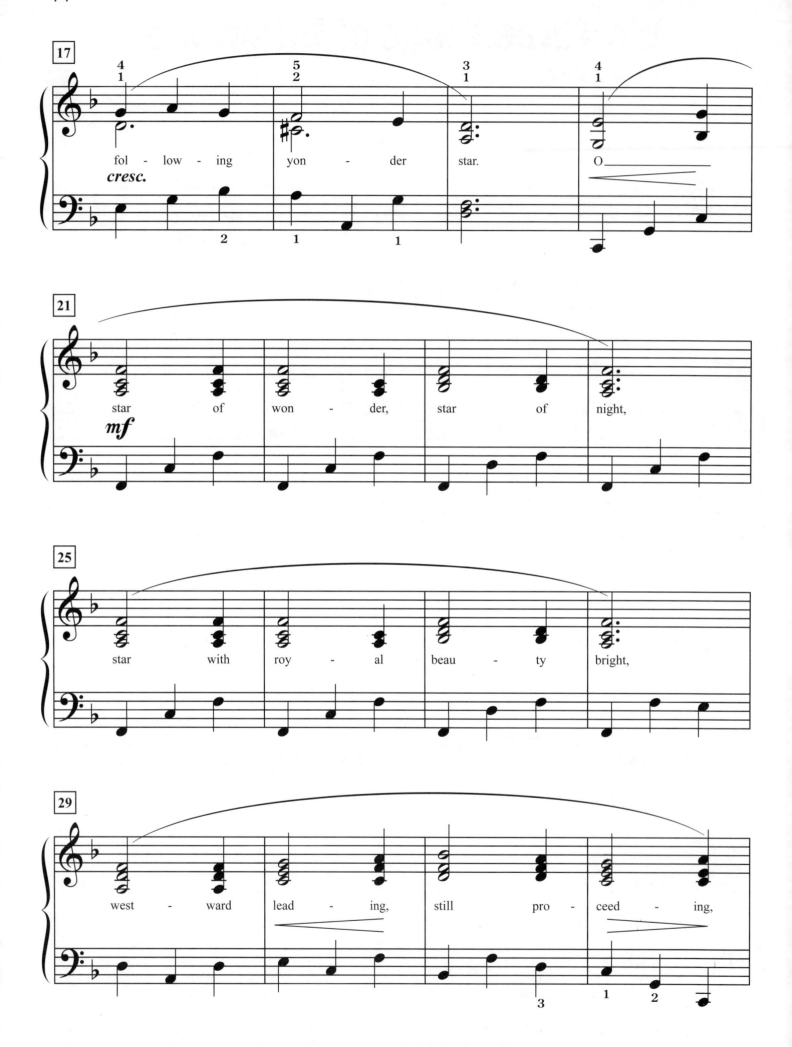

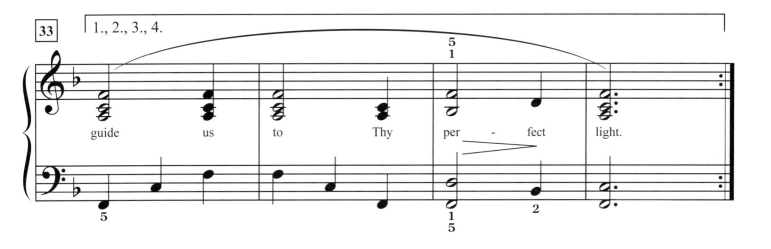

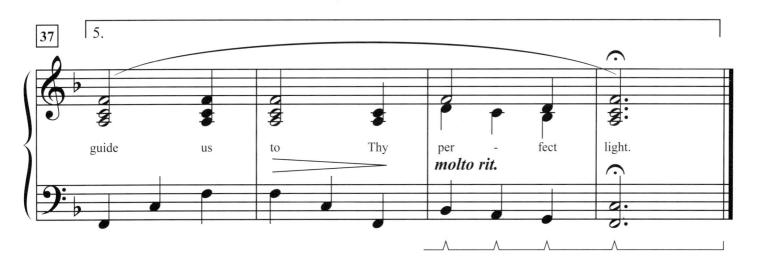

Verse 2:
Born a King on Bethlehem's plain,
Gold I bring, to crown Him again,
King forever, ceasing never
Over us all to reign.
(To Chorus:)

Verse 3:
Frankincense to offer have I,
Incense owns a Deity nigh.
Prayer and praising, all men raising
Worship Him, God most high.
(To Chorus:)

Verse 4:
Myrrh is mine, its bitter perfume
Breathes a life of gathering gloom;
Sorrowing, sighing, bleeding, dying,
Sealed in the stone-cold tomb.
(To Chorus:)

Verse 5:
Glorious now behold Him arise,
King and God and sacrifice.
Alleluia, Alleluia,
Earth to heaven replies.
(To Chorus:)

We Wish You a Merry Christmas

Traditional Carol
Arranged by Dan Coates

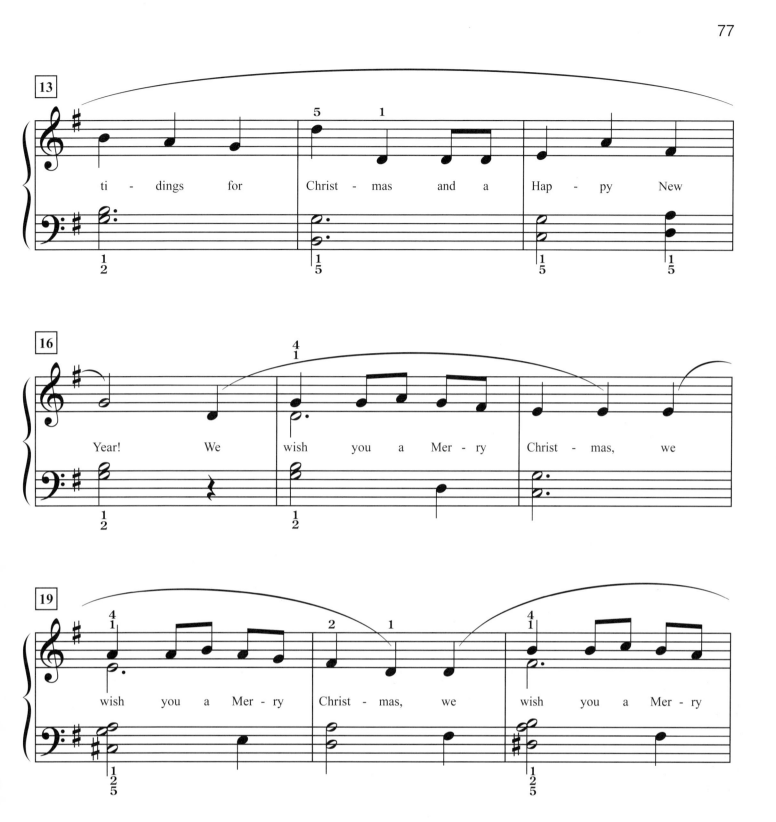

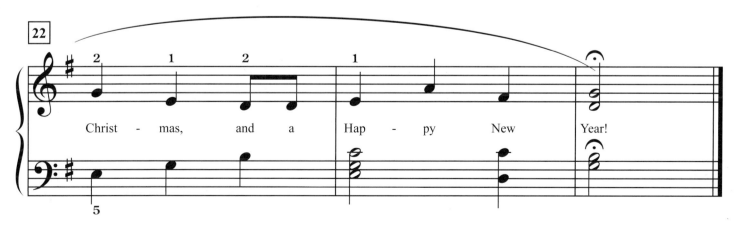

Winter Wonderland

Words by Dick Smith
Music by Felix Bernard
Arranged by Dan Coates

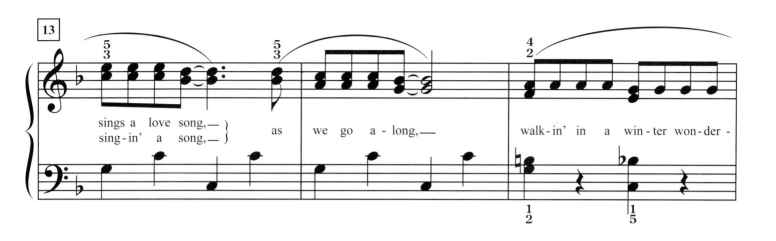

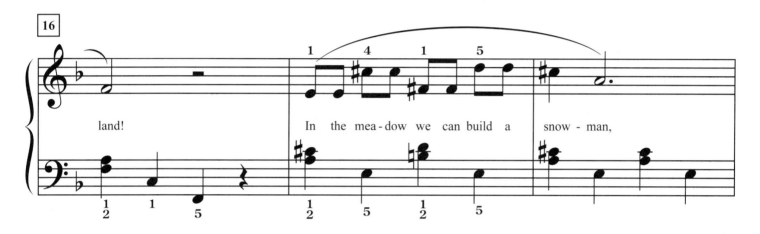

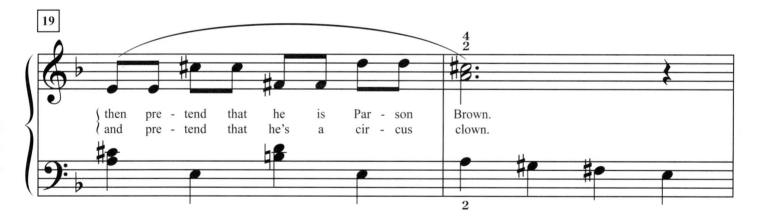

you can do the job when you're in town!" Lat - er
til the oth - er kid - dies knock 'im down! When it

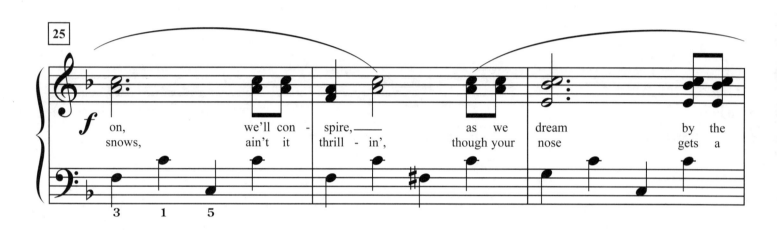

on, we'll con - spire,— as we dream by the
snows, ain't it thrill - in', though your nose gets a

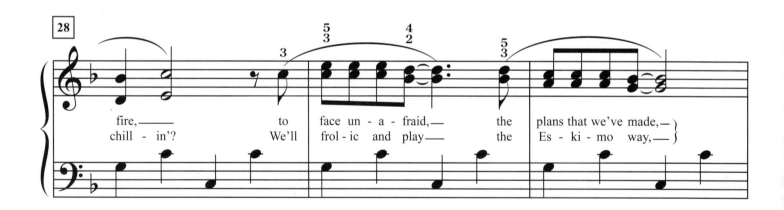

fire,— to face un - a - fraid,— the plans that we've made,—
chill - in'? We'll frol - ic and play— the Es - ki - mo way,—

walk - in' in a win - ter won - der - land! Sleigh bells land!